★HOMELAND

★

NINA
BERMAN

* * T R O L L E Y * *

A LITTLE FABLE

"ALAS," SAID THE MOUSE, "THE WORLD IS GROWING SMALLER EVERY DAY.
AT THE BEGINNING IT WAS SO BIG THAT I WAS AFRAID,
I KEPT RUNNING AND RUNNING, AND I WAS GLAD WHEN AT LAST I SAW WALLS
FAR AWAY TO THE RIGHT AND LEFT, BUT THESE LONG WALLS HAVE NARROWED SO
QUICKLY THAT I AM IN THE LAST CHAMBER ALREADY, AND THERE IN THE CORNER
STANDS THE TRAP THAT I MUST RUN INTO."
"YOU ONLY NEED TO CHANGE YOUR DIRECTION," SAID THE CAT, AND ATE IT UP.

FRANZ KAFKA

★ Law student, pro-Iraq war rally, Times Square, New York City, 2003

★ Camouflage, White House communication team during President Bush's visit to September 11 crash site, Shanksville, Pennsylvania, 2002

★ Homeland Security advisory billboard, one of three in the small town of Country Club Hills, Illinois, 2008

★ Trainee, Citizen Corps/Community Emergency Response team (CERT) session, Union township Fire Station, Winfield, Pennsylvania, 2006

I'm learning how to be safe. I ordered my anti nuke pills and some for my child and a radiation monitor which I put on my key chain. It's cute and looks like a car remote and a bargain at $129. I have a Go kit stashed in a white pail just like the one used by 9-11 rescue heroes during those dark days when they dug through dirt and bones. I'm not sure where I will need to go, but I know someone will tell me.

Meanwhile, I pay attention to the color warnings. A flag in my town flies atop our Homeland Security advisory billboard and lets me know how I should feel each day. When the flag is yellow I'm hopeful about the future and treat myself to a manicure. When it's orange, I'm not so carefree and watch more intently the people around me. With close to one million names on our nation's terrorist watch list, who knows who could be lurking out there?

Take for example, the other morning. I saw a man sitting on a park bench. He had a long dark beard. He wasn't wearing a shirt. I didn't know if he was homeless or an extremist. It seemed odd as he sat there a long time, doing nothing, just watching. I wondered if it was a moment of decision for him. I thought of calling the police "see something, say something," number, but decided against it. That's the tricky thing now. Damned if you do and damned if you don't. I'll just kill myself if I see his picture on the front page of the newspaper one day.

What keeps me going is knowing that even an ordinary person like myself can contribute to the success of the GWOT, that's the Global War On Terror. I work part-time at the nearby military base and dress up like an Iraqi so our troops can practice knowing what to do when they meet real Iraqis.

I belong to the Homefront Security Patrol, a volunteer program that lets me wear a uniform and carry a radio and drive in a police car with a partner three mornings a week. We patrol our streets, public buildings and tennis courts, looking for anything or anyone suspicious - bombs, terrorists, and whatnot.

I organized the last fundraiser in town which raised $1000 for a bulletproof vest for Santos, our canine hero who helps us fight GWOT and WOD, (that's the War On Drugs). I've learned that GWOT and WOD are really the same, because the bad guys trying to kill us with bombs are the very same bad guys harvesting poppies in Afghanistan. I'm a member of Citizen Corps, a program started by our President after 9-11, and we meet once a month. We received a grant for $35,000 for disaster dummies and general upgrades. Next year we'll include Improvised Explosive Devices (IEDs) in the funding requests. That's the new threat concern and also where the big money is, in IEDs, you know, like the ones killing our boys in Iraq.

Later this year, I'm going to take a little trip and spend a week at nuclear war. It will be staged at the old home for the mentally disabled, which the Army bought a few years back when the place went broke. The pay is good - $15 an hour - and I get to practise being rescued. I did that once before when Islamic terrorists attacked our airport, I mean a pretend attack. Really nice fire fighters lifted me into a stretcher and told me everything would be OK. I made a lot of friends that day. I'm thinking nuclear war will be even better. And the people at the defense contractor, which is organizing the victims, said there should be a lot of overtime since it's the first nuclear war and things might be a little chaotic.★

★PREPARE

★ Awaiting rescue, Islamic terrorist nuclear attack simulation, Muscatatuck Urban Training Center, Butlerville, Indiana, 2008

★ A Hazmat team prepares to enter fake shopping mall, Islamic terrorist nuclear attack simulation, Muscatatuck Urban Training Center (MUTC), Butlerville, Indiana. 2007

★ Terrorists attack Midway Airport, "TOPOFF2" Homeland Security $16 million exercise, Chicago, Illinois 2003

★ Bioterror volunteer, pneumonic plague simulation, "TOPOFF2" Homeland Security $16 million exercise, Lake County, Illinois 2003

★ Volunteers, Citizen Corps/Community Emergency Response Team (CERT) session, Union township fire station, Winfield, Pennsylvania, 2006

★ Disaster dummy, Citizen Corps training, Union County fire station, Winfield, Pennsylvania, 2006

★ Potassium iodide distribution, residents arrive to collect free KI pills, part of a national preparedness initiative, Charlotte, North Carolina, 2002

★ Potassium iodide distribution, a woman with her packet of free KI pills, part of a national preparedness initiative, Charlotte, North Carolina, 2002

★ Hazmat team gives thumbs up, Islamic terrorist nuclear attack simulation, Muscatatuck Urban Training Center (MUTC), Butlerville, Indiana, 2007

★ Dog armor, members of the Ladies Auxiliary to the Veterans of Foreign Wars and Santos, the police dog they outfitted with a Kevlar vest, Orange Park, Florida, 2006

★ Injured woman lies on the grass, Islamic terrorist nuclear attack simulation, Muscatatuck Urban Training Center (MUTC), Butlerville, Indiana. 2007

★ Fallout victim, Army veteran, earns $15 an hour playing victim in an Islamic terrorist nuclear attack simulation, MUTC, Butlerville, Indiana. 2007

★ Priority 1, woman lies on the rubble pile waiting to be rescued, Islamic terrorist nuclear attack simulation, Muscatatuck Urban Training Center (MUTC), Butlerville, Indiana, 2007

★ War On Terror goat, one of dozens of farm animals used for GWOT training at a U.S. Army base where daily life in Iraq is simulated, Ft. Polk, Louisiana, 2008

★ Freedom School, a fabricated Iraqi village in "The Box," Joint Readiness Training Center (JRTC), Ft. Polk, Louisiana, 2008

★ Taking cover, role players in "The Box," Joint Readiness Training Center (JRTC), Ft. Polk, Louisiana, 2008

★ Explosion, hired at $12.87 an hour, locals play Iraqis in simulation drills, "The Box," JRTC, Ft. Polk, Louisiana, 2008

★ Woman in burqa serves peanuts, Missionary Day, New Life Church, Colorado Springs, Colorado, 2005

I live in a country uniquely blessed. I feel this when I enter my church and see our Christian flag next to our American flag.

I feel it on God and Country Sunday when members of our military march down the aisle. I'm proud and humbled to have a pastor who is so close to Christ, our warrior, and also to our President.

All the people I know and all the people I work with are members of my church. At 15,000 strong, and growing stronger each day, we are like a small town, neighbor next to neighbor, no one to fear. We are all of one mind and the elders make sure of this by insisting that the sin of homosexuality and other deviations are kept from our midst. I'm comforted to know that around the nation there are so many other churches like ours, with new ones emerging each day.

I go to my church for everything, from worship to aerobics. We read the Bible before crunches. After my workout, I drink a Starbucks, eat a Scripture mint, attend the ladies small group, and visit the bookstore where I can find the latest bestsellers by my pastor and so many others.

Lately, I have been reading books about God and money. I used to think that wealth had nothing to do with faith. Now I know better. God wants me to have nice things. He wants me to drive a new car. He wants me to remodel my kitchen. I only need to believe in Him more, and be more positive in my words. Admittedly, sometimes I'm not sure how to do this. My friend says she does it by imagining herself sitting on Jesus' lap.

Still, it can be perplexing. I had planned a trip to visit my parents who were ill and desperately needed me, but my husband decided the timing wasn't right and said I needed to stay home with our children. I tried to change the plane ticket, but the price had gone up and I didn't have enough money and so I was stuck. Why would God punish me like this? I was crying as I told my story to the ladies in small group. They nodded their heads in sympathy, held my hand, and together we turned to the next chapter of our workbooks. They said Jesus has a plan for all of us and it would be all right. I just needed to pray harder and follow my Bible studies.

There must be something to what they're saying because I look at my church and we've been so blessed. Some weekends we take in $800,000 in offerings. We have a new gym with basketball courts and a workout room (modest attire only). Our pastor lives in a gorgeous large home and has a lovely wife and family. They always look so nice. I adore her earrings.

There are some other books I like to read. My current favorite is the "Left Behind" series and the companion video "Eternal Forces." In the video, the American militia forms an alliance with the Tribulation forces and wages war against the Antichrist's Global Community Peacekeepers. I hope I can pack it along with me when I go on my mission to Yemen. Or is it Kuwait? I'm not sure yet where I'll be sent. Either way it hardly matters, as there are so many Muslims in need of conversion. One of the reasons we're all so pleased about Operation Iraqi Freedom (OIF) and Operation Enduring Freedom (OEF) is that each point of contact between our soldiers and the natives is a chance to spread the word of Christ.

When I think about all the insight I've gained through my church, one thing that really stands out is my understanding of who Christ really is. He is not a limp, effeminate, stained glass sufferer. He is a take charge, alpha male savior. This is what we teach our youth from the time they are babies when they sit in their little high chairs and play pat the Bible. Later, when they're bigger, they go to Bible class taught by a nice man dressed in an Army uniform, who talks about Christ the soldier. Our special sons grow up to become Royal Rangers. I marvel at them dressed in their uniforms with medals and patches, pledging allegiance and offering a salute. Behold, the Royal Rangers as they honor Jesus Christ our Master Ranger.★

★BELIEVE

★ Big Jesus at night, Solid Rock Church, Monroe, Ohio, 2005

Evangelism for the 21s

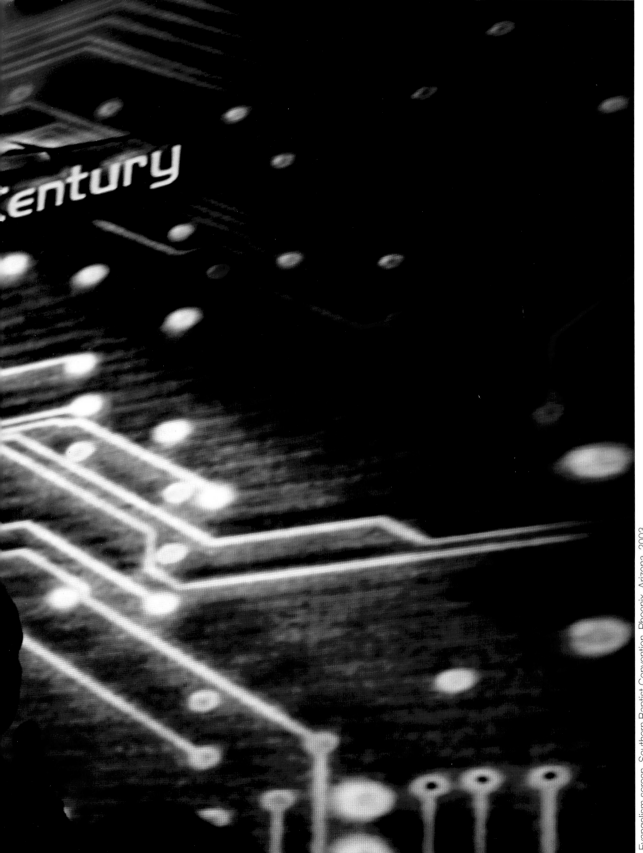

Century

★ Evangelism screen, Southern Baptist Convention, Phoenix, Arizona, 2003

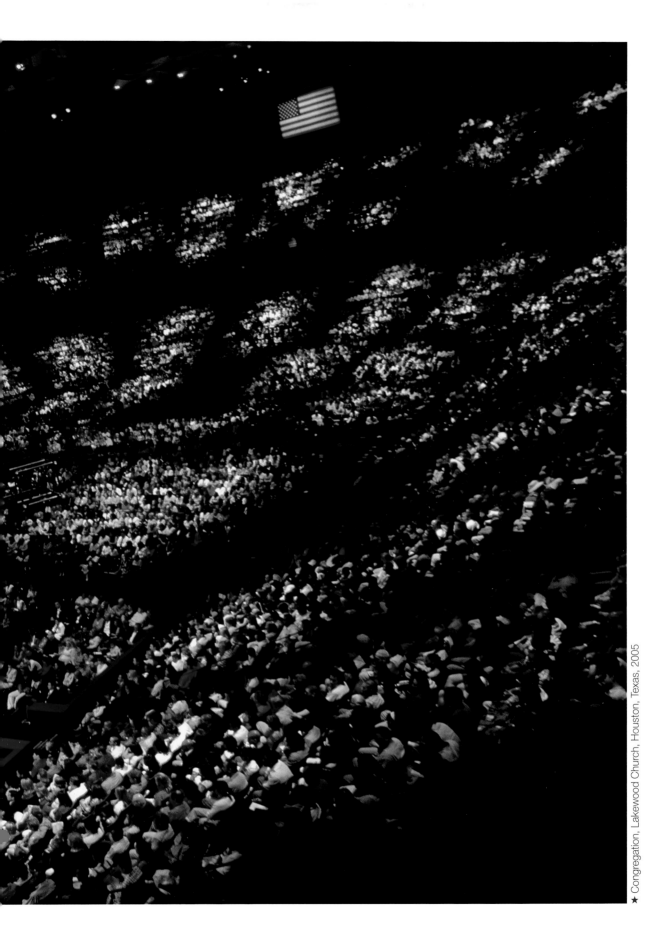

★ Congregation, Lakewood Church, Houston, Texas, 2005

★ Baptismal pool in pink, Southeast Christian Church, Louisville, Kentucky, 2005

★ Church lobby, Southeast Christian Church, Louisville, Kentucky, 2005

★ Woman in burqa serves peanuts, Missionary Day, New Life Church, Colorado Springs, Colorado, 2005

Christian bookstore, Southeast Christian Church, Louisville, Kentucky, 2005

★ Worship Aerobics, New Life Church, Colorado Springs, Colorado, 2005

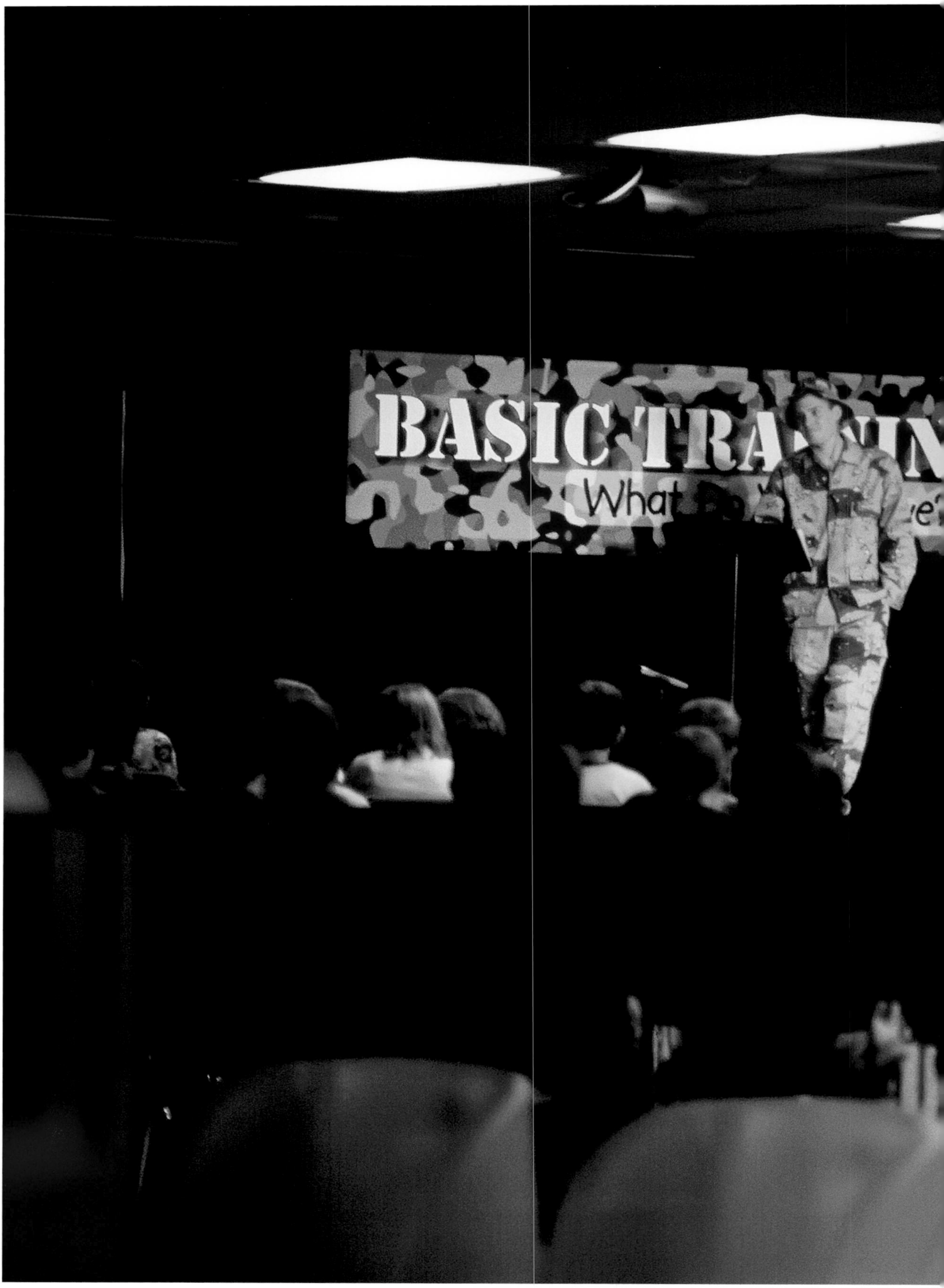
BASIC TRA
What

★ Bible study, Bible studies teacher dressed as an Army soldier in classroom, Southeast Christian Church, Louisville, Kentucky, 2005

★ Royal Ranger salute, Royal Rangers meeting, New Life Church, Colorado Springs, Colorado, 2005

★ Royal Ranger pledge, Royal Rangers meeting, New Life Church, Colorado Springs, Colorado, 2005

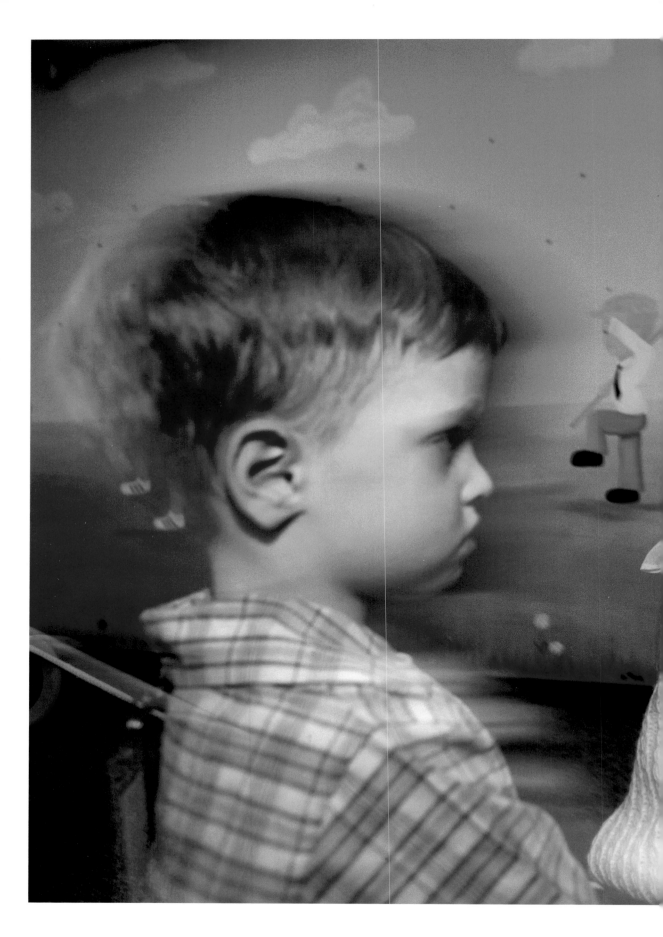

★ Bible school hallway, Southeast Christian Church, Louisville, Kentucky, 2005

★ Boys praying in blue light, New Life Church, Colorado Springs, Colorado, 2005

★ Baptism pool, Southeast Christian Church, Louisville, Kentucky, 2005

★ Pastors Joel and Victoria Osteen on the on-stage screen, Lakewood Church, Houston, Texas, 2005

★ Choir, New Life Church, Colorado Springs, Colorado, 2005

★ Christian couple, Southeast Christian Church, Louisville, Kentucky, 2005

ENTER

★ Worship Center, New Life Church, Colorado Springs, Colorado, 2005

★ Father and son Rangers, New Life Church, Colorado Springs, Colorado, 2005

My President says that somewhere in the world, at this very minute, a terrorist is planning an attack on me.

I think of this and feel scared. And then I feel angry.

On the news I heard that a terrorist was found in a casino in Indiana. Possible terrorists were seen around a church in Illinois. In Arizona, a terrorist plot was foiled involving Afghans, Iraqis and Mexican drug cartels. In Memphis, police and FBI raided dozens of businesses suspected of terrorism. My friend lives in Memphis and she said that the sheriff held a meeting at her church the other night and warned everyone to be on the look out for people taking pictures in public places, because it might really be terrorists scouting targets, which is scary because there are so many targets. I read that a town outside Philadelphia has twenty-four of the possible twenty-five soft targets considered honey to terrorists.

How is it my friends that so many people still don't understand what we're up against?

I thank God for all the boys and girls who sign up each day to fight the GWOT. I saw some the other day at a Marine event at a park near my home. They had cammie colored face paint and were having a nice time touching the rifles and weapons. At one point, Marine attack helicopters flew overhead and I heard the new recruits scream, "This is what Iraq will be like!" I wonder if they also checked out what the Army has to offer. There's this great new game called the Virtual Army Experience. I played it at the Army Strong Zone. I had fun killing bad guys with a stinger.

I'm also grateful to our police departments, which are the first line of our Homeland defense. I see them training hard to learn military-style tactics and weapons because who knows when or where a terrorist

could appear. Some people complain that all the gear they need to buy - the new weapons, the bomb dogs, the bulletproof vests for the dogs, the grenade launchers, the gas masks, the special boats, the air-conditioned trucks and decontamination suits - is too expensive, but how can you put a value on a life potentially saved? The way it was explained to me, which makes a lot of sense, goes like this: If a terrorist is on a boat and the boat is armed with explosives, and the terrorist is going to ram that boat into a crowd of people on shore, don't you want the police to have the highest-powered, most accurate weapons available on the planet, not to mention a really fast boat, to take that terrorist out? And maybe not just one weapon, but two or three in case one jams.

If we want our police to go head-to-head with Al Qaeda operatives, I want to be sure they have all they need to get the guys dead, and to do it now, not next week. And to be honest, when I think of all the hardship and suffering these terrorists have caused us, I wouldn't mind if some pain was inflicted in the process.★

★ Little Patriots, July 4, Ridgefield Park, New Jersey, 2003

★ Give war a chance, bumper sticker on a Marine's pick-up truck, Washington, Illinois, 2006

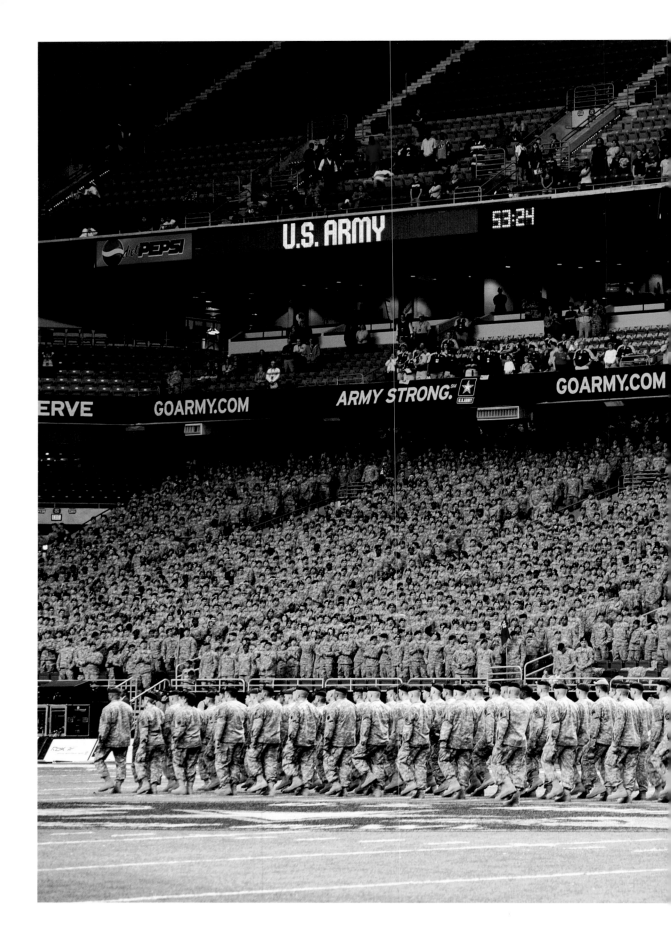

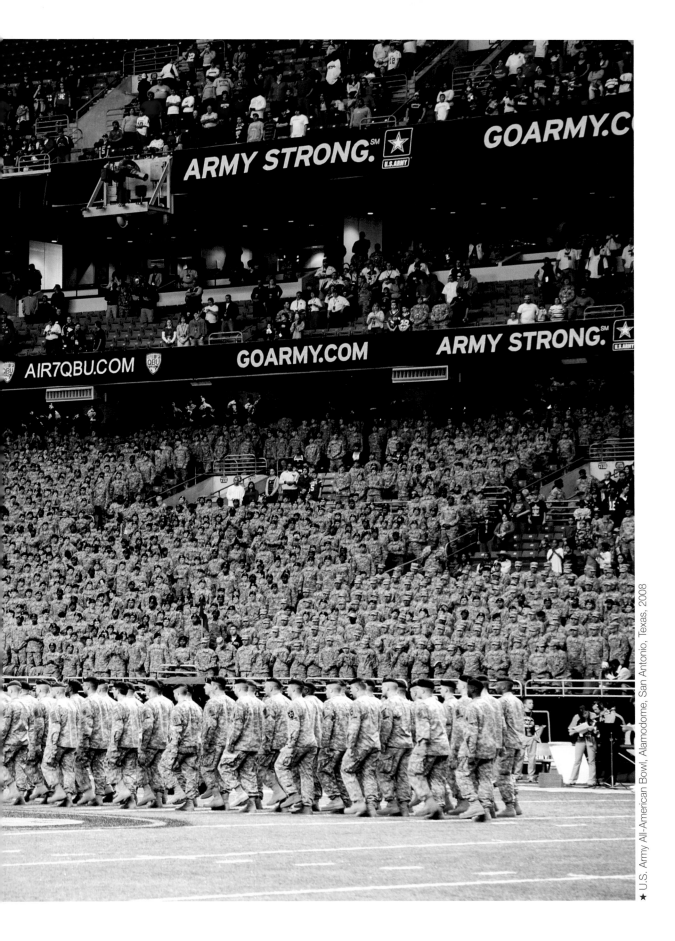

★ U.S. Army All-American Bowl, Alamodome, San Antonio, Texas, 2008

★ Girl, Army Strong Zone, outside the Alamodome, San Antonio, Texas, 2008

★ Boy, Army Strong Zone, outside the Alamodome, San Antonio, Texas, 2008

★ Human target practice, All-America day with the 82nd Airborne, Ft. Bragg, North Carolina, 2006

★ Helicopter flyby, All-America day with the 82nd Airborne, Ft. Bragg, North Carolina, 2006

★ Marine helicopter, U.S. Marines in attack helicopters fly over Orchard Beach to simulate a raid, The Bronx, New York, 2007

★ Marine weapons display, Orchard Beach, The Bronx, New York, 2007

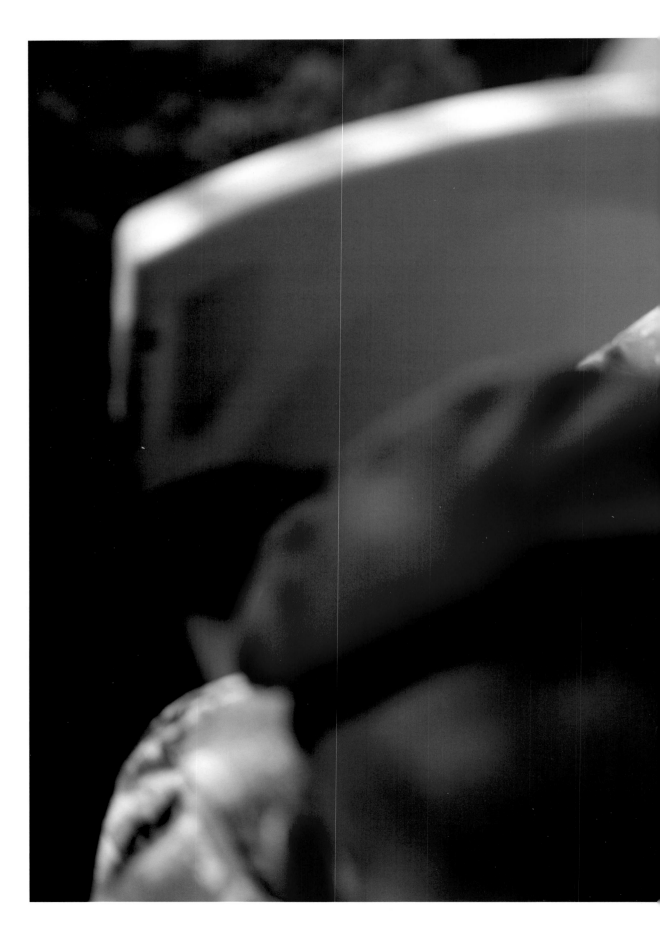

★ Face painting, All-America day with the 82nd Airborne, Ft. Bragg, North Carolina, 2006

★ Marines weapons display, Orchard Beach, The Bronx, New York, 2007

★ Marines weapons display, Orchard Beach, the Bronx, New York, 2007

★ Marine Day, Times Square, New York City, 2007

★ Children in military riot gear, on board the Navy battleship Wasp during Fleet Week festivities, New York City, 2007

★ Window display, Future Warrior shop, downtown Fayetteville, North Carolina, 2006

★ Soldiers on red carpet, Columbus Day parade, held the day after the first bombing of Afghanistan, New York City, 2001

★ Marching practice, Oakland Military Institute, a public school funded by the Pentagon, Oakland, California, 2003

★ Medal ceremony, Oakland Military Institute, a public school funded by the Pentagon, Oakland, California, 2003

★ Special Weapons And Tactics (SWAT) police at the annual SWAT Round-Up, Orlando, Florida, 2006

★ SWAT Round-Up, Orlando, Florida, 2006

★ SWAT Round-Up, Orlando, Florida, 2006

★ SWAT Round-Up, Orlando, Florida, 2006

★ SWAT Round-Up, terrorist hunting permit, Orlando, Florida, 2006

★ SWAT Round-Up, obstacle course, Orlando, Florida, 2006

★ SWAT Round-Up, obstacle course, Orlando, Florida, 2006

★ SWAT Round-Up, obstacle course, Orlando, Florida, 2006

★ SWAT Round-Up, obstacle course, Orlando, Florida, 2006

★ Big Jesus, Solid Rock Church, Monroe, Ohio, 2005

★ President Bush, Focus on the Family movie theater, Colorado Springs, Colorado, 2005

★ Border wall, a stretch of the new Homeland Security border wall costing $3million a mile, Naco, Arizona, 2008

★ Confiscated goods, a state worker tags items collected from airport checkpoints. The items, considered dangerous for air travel, are put on eBay and sold for a profit, Harrisburg, Pennsylvania, 2008

★ Shop window, New York City, 2003

★ Suburban home, Ridgefield Park, New Jersey, 2006

★ Stealth Bomber, Atlantic City, New Jersey, 2007

★ Border Watch, contemplating the "Mexican invasion" a member of a citizen's Border Watch group at home with his dogs. Arizona – Mexico border, USA, 2008

★ Insurgent dummies, dummies used for military training scenarios in Iraq and Afghanistan, Ft. Polk, Louisiana, 2008

★ Al-Qaeda sign, "The Box," Joint Readiness Training Center (JRTC), Ft. Polk, Louisiana, 2008

★ Fargo, North Dakota, 2003

My concern is that, years from now, people will study Nina Berman's pictorial chronicle of the American "security state," spanning the first decade of the twenty-first century, and draw an all-too-straightforward connection between these scenes and the 2001 destruction of the World Trade Towers, the attack on the Pentagon and the ensuing anthrax scare.

Doing so, however, would assume that this imagery documented the American public's hysterical reaction to incomprehensible events - as opposed to a more manipulated reaction based on the U.S. government's opportunistic employment of fear.

But then, who could imagine – unless you lived through it, but even then! – the induced hallucination of paranoia and mad outrage unleashed by a renegade troupe led by director Richard Cheney, producer Karl Rove and their "helpless-without-cue cards" lead actor, George W. Bush.

If there is a more understandable political subtext to Nina's fantastical images and the callow aching madness that still resonates across the American landscape, it is how Osama bin Laden's insanity so perfectly engaged the extreme narcissism and susceptibility-toward-slight of America's cowboy-President. Bush, after all, has never made any bones over the fact that this attack on America (by a supposedly nameless, faceless, extremist Islam) came to instantly represent his reason for being.

Sadly, with the American media only now loosening its grip on the pom-poms, what has been irretrievably lost is any chance to differentiate and understand the effects of the deadly 9/11 attack free-and-clear of the miasma of Bush's own holy war, the "Global War On Terror"; the intimidation of Congress and the press; the suspension of habeas corpus; the maintenance of secret offshore prisons; the willful employment of torture; the massive war profiteering; and the crucifixion

of Iraq in the name of "Homeland Security," democratic values, moral goodness - and changing the subject.

Even - or maybe, especially - in the waning days of this presidential administration, it seems impossible to believe that a divorce will finally take place between Homeland and Bushland. This "incredulity," and the deep trauma surrounding it, is the true testament of this book. Because, what these pages contain is nothing short of a visceral grand tour of how "the events of September 11, 2001," the goodwill of the American people, and the Bush Administration's appropriation of terror became indelibly shrink-wrapped.★

MICHAEL
SHAW,
PH.D.

I made these photographs between 2001 and 2008. They were taken all across the United States.

The title of the book comes from President George W. Bush, who introduced the word "homeland" shortly after September 11. Previously unfamiliar in American speech, the word sounded both sinister and soothing filled with ideological import of mysterious origin. Was it British, or maybe Nazi Germany? Or was the word drawn from fiction, a made-up world existing in a fairytale?

This name is now our place, which we occupy and define. We have assigned roles that are played out everyday.

In my photographs, Homeland is where Air Force bombers entertain sunbathers on summer weekends; happy families step through the suburbs clutching anti-nuke pills; small town police train to hunt terrorists; evangelical Christians dress in Afghan burqas; senior citizens become extras in a War On Terror script; and military recruitment spectacles transform children into would-be killers.

All across the country there are frequent simulation drills costing millions of dollars and involving thousands of participants where various war scenarios are imagined: Islamic terrorists with nuclear bombs, Islamic terrorists hijacking planes, bioterrorists, chemical terrorists, school bus terrorists and shopping mall terrorists. There is even a camp for wayward youth to help them learn how to respond to terrorists.

Some of these events have the look and feel of state-sponsored performance art, where realism is replaced by theater, giving participants a powerful sense of identity and value through a militarized experience. It is this identity and the ambiguity between real and made-up, so emblematic of post 9-11 discourse, that interests me most.

I came to this project while photographing very graphic examples of the human cost of war. Several of the wounded soldiers I met said they grew up thinking that war would be "fun" and remembered watching the first Gulf War on TV which they described as "awesome."

Rather than continuing to focus on the evidence of war, it seemed important for me to show the fantasies of war.

I made these images mindful of my own conflicted response to the call for "Homeland Security." I would wake up some mornings in Manhattan wondering if I should take the subway and then berate myself for being fearful; I would laugh at the preparedness kits offered on the Internet and then shamefully buy them. I abhor the idea of racial profiling but once found myself looking suspiciously at an Arab man who sat silently for several hours on a park bench near my home.

It occurred to me that my feelings and fears could take me in any direction, if the conditions were right. Once you buy into something, everything else falls into place, creating a certainty that can be quite consuming.

I longed for a speaker – other than our elected officials - who exemplified this certainty, and so I created one. The narrator of Homeland is a fictional creation drawn from real life conversations I've had with people I photographed or spoke with, details of scenes I witnessed, news reports and on a few occasions, my own musings.

To some, the narrator will seem over the top and not to be believed. I urge the reader to consider a different interpretation. ★

★HOMELAND

NINA BERMAN

My thanks to Gigi Giannuzzi, friend, publisher,
and patron saint to photographers the world over.

To Michael Shaw, for his words and genius.

Additional thanks to writer Andrea Boehm who
accompanied me to church; photo editors
Monica Allende, Ruth Eichorn and Hillary Raskin
who supported the work; and my dear friends,
Sue Brisk, Stephen Ferry and Sandra Roa for
their conversations and help in editing.

Special love and appreciation goes to my partner
Carmine Galasso who always encouraged my
trips and our daughter Carla, for her smile when
I would return.

Published in Great Britain in 2008
By Trolley Ltd
www.trolleybooks.com

Photographs © Nina Berman 2008
Texts © Michael Shaw, Nina Berman
Creative Direction: Gigi Giannuzzi
Art Direction: Martin & Wai,
www.fruitmachinedesign.com
Text Editing: Hannah Watson

The right of Nina Berman to be identified as the
author of this work has been asserted by her
in accordance with the copyright, designs and
patents act 1998.

A catalogue record for this book is available from
the British Library.

ISBN 978-1-904563-72-3

Printed in Italy by Grafiche Antiga 2008.

★ACKNOWLEDGEMENTS★